PLAY BALL, SNOOPY

by CHARLES M. SCHULZ

Selected cartoons from
WIN A FEW, LOSE A FEW, CHARLIE BROWN, Vol. 1

FAWCETT CREST • NEW YORK

PLAY BALL, SNOOPY

This book, prepared especially for Fawcett Crest Books,
a unit of CBS Publications, the Consumer Publishing
Division of CBS Inc., comprises the first half of WIN A FEW,
LOSE A FEW, CHARLIE BROWN and is reprinted by
arrangement with Holt, Rinehart and Winston, Inc.

Copyright © 1973, 1974 by United Feature Syndicate, Inc.

ALL RIGHTS RESERVED.

ISBN 0-449-23222-0

Printed in the United States of America

16   15   14   13

PLAY BALL, SNOOPY

GOOD MORNING, MISS... I'M SELLING A NEW ITEM FOR KITTENS, AND I..

FOR WHAT?

FOR KITTENS...THIS IS A NEW TOY I HAVE DEVELOPED...A KITTEN CAN ENTERTAIN HIMSELF FOR HOURS WITH THIS TOY...

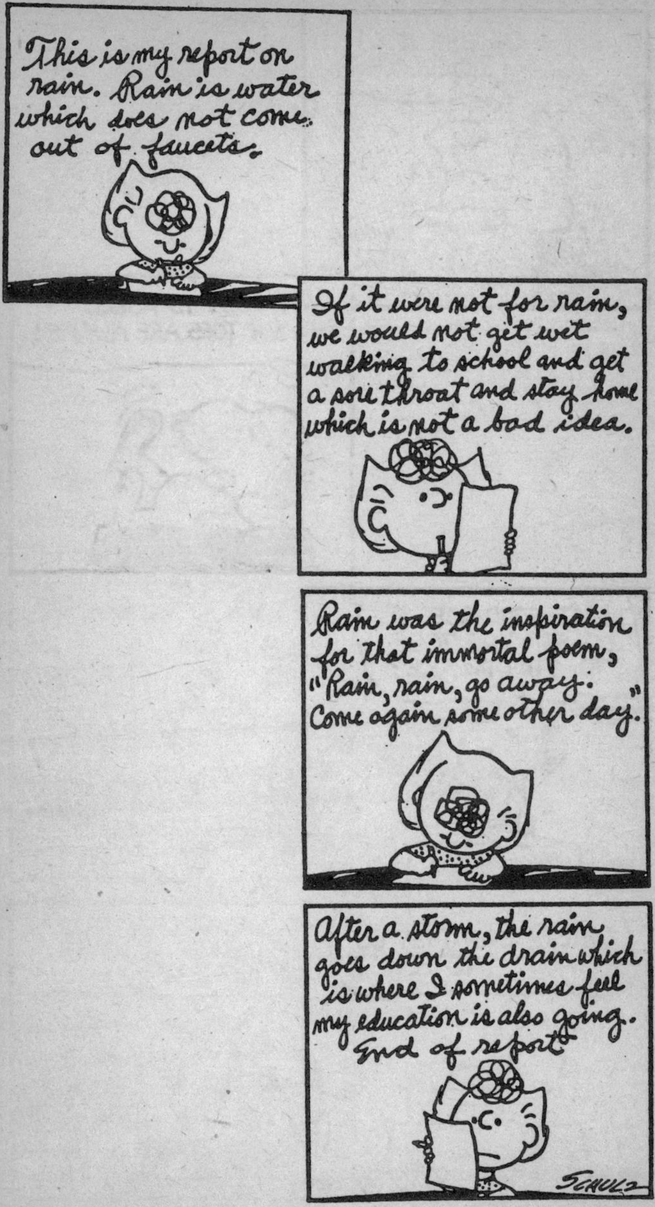
This is my report on rain. Rain is water which does not come out of faucets.
If it were not for rain, we would not get wet walking to school and get a sore throat and stay home which is not a bad idea.
Rain was the inspiration for that immortal poem, "Rain, rain, go away. Come again some other day."
After a storm, the rain goes down the drain which is where I sometimes feel my education is also going. End of report.
SCHULZ

ZIP!

MORE PEANUTS®

(in editions with brightly colored pages)

☐ A BOY NAMED CHARLIE BROWN   23217 $2.25

☐ SNOOPY AND HIS SOPWITH CAMEL   23799 $1.75

☐ SNOOPY AND THE RED BARON   23719 $1.75

☐ THE "SNOOPY, COME HOME"
  MOVIE BOOK   23726 $1.95